BURNING BUSH
——— BOOKS ———

Charlotte,
Your heart matters to God. You are
the apple of His eye and He longs for
you to draw closer to Him. Experience
a time of refreshing and healing as you
sit at His feet. Destiny awaits. You're
too full to be empty!

TOO FULL TO BE EMPTY

Adrienne Mayfield, Esq.

BURNING BUSH
BOOKS

BURNING BUSH BOOKS

Too Full To Be Empty

Published by Burning Bush Books

Copyright © 2021 by Adrienne Mayfield

First edition May 2021

For information about bulk purchases, please contact Adrienne Mayfield at:

amayfield2147@gmail.com.

Manufactured in the United States of America

ISBN: 978-0-9997694-8-5

All Scripture quotations, unless otherwise noted, taken from the Holy Bible, New King James Version.

Cover Design: Adrienne Mayfield

Cover Image: Desy Suryani

Visit the author's website at **adriennemayfield.com**

This book is dedicated to women who are seeking purpose and significance

Table of Contents

Introduction

One of the greatest benefits of being a child of God is knowing that we are promised abundant life. Jesus said, "I have come that they may have life and that they may have it more abundantly." John 10:10. This promise in Scripture does not relate to the sweet by and by, as many think and teach, but it is a guarantee that a relationship with Jesus promises a better life here on Earth. Despite this promise, however, the full measure of all Christ died to give us often eludes us. We find ourselves seeking peace and contentment in things that are fleeting. We are left empty and broken as a result. It is true, though, that this is not God's desire for us. Therefore, you should at least try to see how you can attain the blessings that you are promised.

You owe it to yourself and your destiny to walk out the fullness of all you are created to be. It is fruitless to dull your shine and act insignificant because of the insecurities of others.

You are created and uniquely fashioned for a destiny and purpose. You are endowed with talents, abilities, and skills that have the potential to solve a problem and transform the world. Refusing to explore the depth of your potential is an insult to the God who created you, and it leaves you unfulfilled. You know it deep inside. You cannot hide it. Despite your best attempts to go with the flow and just go with the status quo, inherently, you already know the truth. You are too full to be empty!

Chapter 1

Eve- Falling for The Lies of the Enemy

Genesis 3:1-20

Despite our own best attempts to hear from God and our biblical knowledge, we often try to do what we believe to be in our best interest. We find it difficult to silence the voices of naysayers who encourage us against following what God has said. We forget to pause and listen for the still, small voice before we make any decision. We foolishly follow the way of Eve and listen to the lying allure of the serpent. We get tempted to listen to his lies rather than trust and rely with confidence on what God has spoken or revealed in His Word.

Eve's emptiness came from believing the lies of the enemy. Eve was not blind or ignorant about God's command. God's instructions were clear, "Of the tree of the knowledge of good and evil, you shall not eat . . ." Genesis 2:17. When the serpent approached Eve, he attempted to negate what God had spoken. He encouraged Eve to question God's motivation and the sincerity of His heart. He tried to make her believe God's boundaries were unfair and set up to hold her down.

Many times, when we read about Adam and Eve, we judge them for their disobedience and criticize them for believing a lie. What about you and me? Are we falling for the same trick of the enemy? Have we eaten the forbidden fruit of rebellion and disobedience to God's law? Do we ever refuse to do what God has commanded because we believe we know what is best?

We often find it challenging to comprehend how someone would willingly choose to believe a lie. Yet, we allow the enemy to convince us that he is our friend, that he is to be trusted, and that God is a liar. We fall for the lies and deception of the enemy time and time again, aborting our destiny by willfully sinning against God. The result is always disastrous.

It's time that we begin to think about what we've been thinking about. We need to consider what is actually feeding our souls and the choices we are making. We often get caught up thinking that God is withholding something from us when he doesn't give us the things that we think that we need. For some reason, we believe we know better.

The enemy has a unique and crafty way of convincing us that God is withholding his favor and blessings, so we foolishly try to implement our own plan. In Genesis 3, we find Eve and her interaction with the serpent. He approaches her with one simple question asking, "Has God indeed said that you shall not eat of every tree of the garden?" Genesis 3:3. This interaction teaches us about the danger of engaging in conversation with Satan.

We must all remember that Satan is a fallen angel. He hung around the throne of God before the fall. Therefore, he is well-equipped to influence and deceive us. Before we know it, we will be doing things that we should not do.

His ultimate goal is to make us disobey God and break His heart. If we ever doubt Satan's ability, we need only look at the fact that he was able to convince one-third of the angels to join him in forming a coup against the Most High God.

Although they were unsuccessful and were thrown out of heaven into Earth, the important point is that through Satan's manipulation, he was able to convince them to disobey God. Thus, it is foolish to think we possess the ability to withstand and defeat him in and of our own strength.

Anytime we began to embark into a conversation with him or entertain thoughts he puts into our own mind, we set ourselves up for a fall. We have to rely on the wisdom and discernment of the Holy Spirit to defeat Satan so we are not deceived. Second Corinthians 2:11 reminds us of the possibilities if we are naïve. "Lest Satan should take advantage of us; for we are not ignorant of his devices." Reliance on our strength or intellect can be fatal. In Eve's case, Satan simply removed one word from the truth and instruction God gave them. He was able to convince Eve and Adam to abort their purpose and relinquish the authority and dominion God had given them.

We must be on guard from the enemy. Thus is the importance of reading and knowing the Word of God. When someone in a bank is being trained to recognize counterfeit money, she is given real money to study. One might think it would be more helpful to study fake money, but the opposite is true. To discern the genuine, we must study the real, not the counterfeit. Such is the same with God. To understand God's nature, to be skilled in recognizing the voice of the enemy, we must know and recognize God. One of the primary ways to learn God's ways is through his Word. As you study and familiarize yourself with the ways He has operated in the past, you will be blessed and armed with a very valuable piece of artillery—TRUTH. Truth is an impenetrable defense against lies.

Any word that contradicts Scripture, any idea that seeks to elevate itself above the supremacy of Scripture must be cast down. Second Corinthians 10:5 tells us that we must learn to cast down every imagination and every high thing that exalts itself against the knowledge of God, bringing it into captivity to the obedience of Christ. This is the key to victory!

When you learn to guard your mind and submit every thought to God, you will begin to only allow ideas that support God's plan and idea for your life to take root in you. You will refuse anything that seeks to destroy you or interrupt divine providence in your life.

Learn from Eve. Do not entertain the lies of the enemy. Believe and speak only what God has said. Cling to what is righteous. Hold onto what is good. Submit to the perfect will of God for your life and trust Him with your entire life. Give Him your dreams; release your pain to Him, and trust His perfect plan. Reject every lie of the enemy and fight for the plan that God has for your life. You are too full to be empty!

Questions:

1. What is something the enemy has offered you to turn your heart from God?

2. How can you discern whether an idea, thought or suggestion is really from God?

3. What can you do if you discover that you have believed a lie?

4. Have you ever accused God of withholding something good from you? What was the outcome?

5. When someone says that God is your Father, how does that make you feel?

6. Pray this. Father, help me recognize your voice. May I never be tricked by the deception of the enemy. Keep me in your perfect will. Amen.

Chapter 2

Sarai-Substituting God's Plan for My Own
Genesis 16:1-6

Sarai is married to Abraham. God promised them that they would have a child, but they are growing old. As a matter of fact, when God spoke it to her, she laughed. She heard the promise, but Sarai's patience is wearing thin. So, here she sits, attempting to come up with an alternative plan. How many times have we done the same? We know God has something in mind for us. We sense it. He has spoken it, but we are tired of waiting. We decide to help God by coming up with an alternative—what a terrible idea!

Sarai's plan is one that we might find surprising. She suggests that Abraham sleep with her servant Hagar.

Somehow, she believes that she can help God deliver the promise. Abraham goes along with the idea, and Hagar becomes pregnant. As expected, Sarai begins to resent her. Think about it. It was Sarai's idea after all. Now, likely, the very sight of Hagar angers her. Hagar's bulging stomach is a reminder of the promise Sarai has that has not been fulfilled. We often fall into this trap. We compare ourselves with other women and bemoan the fact that they have something we think should belong to us. Jealousy and envy take over and block God's ability to bless us the way He desires to.

Sarai goes to Abraham. She complains that Hagar despises her, and she pushes Abraham to do something. Abraham acquiesces and tells her she can do whatever she wishes. Sarai deals harshly with her, and Hagar runs away.

Sarai's story teaches us that we can never improve on God's plan. When we attempt to help God or do something outside of His timing, disaster results. We must learn to be patient and wait for his Divine answer. We must trust that He will deliver on His promise. We get into big trouble when we try to do things our own way. We don't need to help God. We only need to submit to his authority and obey. Learning to wait on God and trust Him is one of the most important things you can learn to do.

Has there been a time when you failed to wait on God? A time when you got really anxious and jumped ahead of him? I am certain you have the battle scars from that experience. Trusting God is an important principle in our growth and development. God has a proven track record that he can be trusted. The Bible reminds us, "God is not a man, that He should lie, nor a son of man, that He should repent. Has He said, and will He not do? Or has He spoken, and will He not make it good? Numbers 23:19. God never makes a mistake, and He never makes a promise He cannot fulfill.

One of the most difficult things about growing in our walk with God is learning to be patient, but our impatience proves that we do not really understand the heart of God. It shows that we fail to comprehend the depth of His great love for us. If we truly understood how much God loves us and how much He wants to bless us as his children, we would never doubt his intentions. We would never doubt the integrity of waiting for the manifestation of the things that He has promised.

Our God longs to speak to us. He longs to bless us, and He alone is faithful. Whenever you doubt God's plan for your life, if ever you wonder if He sees you and plans to work things out in your life, remember Sarai. She got ahead of God and came up with her own plan, but God blessed her just like He promised. God can be trusted. He will not leave you wanting. Every promise He has made to you will be fulfilled. You must only persevere and trust Him. Don't turn to your own devices. Don't stop believing. Trust in the only one who can help you. You are too full to be empty!

Questions:

1. When have you felt that God was taking too long?

2. How did you respond?

3. How can we learn to patiently wait on God for answers to our prayers?

4. Has there been a time when you rushed God's plan and regretted your impatience?

5. What are you waiting for God to do for you now?

6. Pray this. Father, your plan is always best. I will wait on you to answer my prayers. Teach me to trust you with my future. Amen.

Chapter 3

Hagar-Finding Peace as A Single Mother

Genesis 16

The story of Hagar is one that is quite interesting. We learned about Hagar in the previous chapter as Sarai's handmaiden. We also learned that because of Sarai's impatience, Hagar was forced to sleep with Abraham. Once she became pregnant, contention arose between her and Sarai. This part of the story is not at all a hard sell to believe or comprehend. Two women in the same house being intimate with the same man .. . It's the drama soap operas are made of, right?

17

Hagar is helpless in this situation. When she is ordered to sleep with her master, she must comply. Now, there she sits, pregnant and likely resented by the very one who put her in this predicament. Frustrated, she runs away. We pick up with her story in Genesis 16. The Angel of the Lord finds her by a spring in the wilderness. He asks why she is there, and she tells Him that she has fled from her mistress. The Lord tells her she must return and submit to Sarai. He also tells her that her descendants will be multiplied through the son she carries.

He also gives her a prophecy about the child she is carrying, "Behold, you are with child, and you shall bear a son. You shall call his name, Ishmael, because the Lord has heard your affliction. He shall be a wild man; His hand shall be against every man, And every man's hand against him. And he shall dwell in the presence of all his brethren." Genesis 16:11-12. After Hagar's encounter with God, she refers to God as El Roi, which means "I have seen the God who sees me."

What about you? Do you feel seen by God or even those around you? Have you ever been placed in a situation beyond your control then judged or misused as a result? This was the case with Hagar, and many women have a similar experience. Perhaps you were molested or raped. Perhaps you were forced to use your body in a way that made you feel used and discarded. Maybe you were impregnated as a result. Maybe you made a decision that landed you in a very difficult place. Perhaps you have lost someone very close to you or you have been attempting to conceive without success. There are many things that come to test our faith, but do not despair.

Take comfort in the story of Hagar. Even if you are placed in a bad situation through no fault of your own, you are running for your life, if you try to run away from His presence, or try to fix things on your own, God will seek after you. You were purchased for an expensive price, and He will leave the 99 just for you. If you feel rejected, forgotten or misunderstood, cry out for El Roi, the God who sees. Even if it appears no one else understands or sees you, He does. If you seek Him, He will be found, and he will find a way to take the mistakes and negative experiences in your life and make them beautiful. The Bible tells us that He has made all things beautiful in His time. Ecclesiastes 3:11.

Allow the story of Hagar to remind you that we have a God who sees us, knows us, and wants to be known. I don't know exactly what may have happened to you, but I do know that nothing is big enough to keep God from you. Nothing can separate you from the love of God. At all times in your life, seek the face and presence of the God who sees. He will give you beauty for ashes. Do not attempt to do life on your own. You are too full to be empty!

Questions:

1. **Think of a time when you felt abandoned. Did you attempt to bring God into the situation?**

2. **How does knowing God as El Roi change your perspective of him.**

3. **What name would you give God for coming through for you in a time of crisis?**

4. **Create a list of five things God has done in your life. Post them on your refrigerator or mirror as a**

daily reminder of his faithfulness. He is the God who sees.

Chapter 4

Lot's Wife-The Danger of Refusing to Move Forward

Genesis 19:12-26

There's a scripture that tells us that no man who puts his hand to the plow and looks back is fit for the kingdom of God. Luke 9:62. Scripture also reminds us that once we begin a forward motion, we should set our eyes to look forward to our future. It can be disastrous to turn to look back at something God has taken from us. Gazing or longing for our past can keep us from moving forward and set us up for disastrous results.

God is the God of our future. He sees the end from the beginning, and He is Alpha and Omega. He is always looking to do something new and fresh. Do not try to box him in! In Isaiah 43:19, He says, "Behold, I will do a new thing, now it shall spring forth; Shall you not know it? I will even make a road in the wilderness and rivers in the desert."

God always desires to move us forward into the future he has planned for us. Before you were ever created, God had a purpose in mind for you. In fact, your purpose was on the mind of God before He actually put you into your mother's womb. Jeremiah 29:11 tells us, "I know the thoughts and plans I have for you, plans to prosper you and not to harm you, to give you a hope and future." An understanding of God's perfect plan solidifies our confidence and trust in God so we will not fear what is ahead.

Lot's wife made the disastrous decision to look back. The angels that came to escort her family told Lot that they had come to destroy the city because of the tremendous outcry against sin that had come up to God. Lot and his

24

family hesitate, so the angels grab them by their hands to lead them out of the city. How many times has God had to pull you out of dangerous situations? Are you someone who walks in wisdom? Do you quickly turn away from things that could cause you danger or do you have to be pulled out? The answer to these questions is something you need to consider because hesitation and disobedience can sometimes be fatal.

As Lot and his family arrive outside the city, the angel says, "Escape for your life! Do not look back behind you nor stay anywhere in the plain. Escape to the mountains, lest you be destroyed." Genesis 19:17. The angel's instructions are crystal clear, and even the resulting consequence is shared as an additional deterrent.

It seems like such a simple instruction. Lot and his family know that Sodom and Gomorrah are about to be destroyed. They know that the angel is trying to save their lives. Thus, it is confusing that as they reach safety in Zoar, Lot's wife looks back and becomes a pillar of salt. Such was the allure of her former life that she found it impossible to move forward without glancing back.

Unfortunately, Lot's wife makes the mistake that many of us make; she finds her past irresistible. Verse 26 tells us, "But his wife looked back behind him, and she became a pillar of salt." Lot's wife remains unnamed, and she is remembered as the woman who just had to look back.

Perhaps she was curious about what was happening, you might say. Maybe she just wanted one last look. We will never know her motivation. We can never hear from her again because right then, right there, she became a pillar of salt. She mortgaged her future for a glance at her past, and the pillar of salt remains in her place today. Stuck in time. Frozen. Destiny aborted. Forever.

There have been so many times in my personal life when I have been tempted to go back to something I didn't need. Many times, it was a refusal to leave something that I knew was hurting me. Fear tries to make us drawback, and bondage invites us to stay in an unhealthy cycle. Familiarity can seem safer than the unknown, but I have learned that the unknown with God is much more secure than any comfort I think I have found in a familiar place.

We must be strong and wise enough to trust God and move forward. We must learn to walk away.

Learn from Lot's wife. When God moves you forward, do not look back. You might be tempted to fear or draw back. Don't do it. Trust that a closed door means it is time to focus on something else. Trust the God who knows the end from the beginning. He never fails. You can never move forward if you keep looking back. You must break the cycle and temptation to stay stuck in the past. Push past your fear and keep moving. You are too full to be empty!

Questions:

1. Have you ever been afraid to go forward into something new? Why?

2. What or who keeps you from going "all in" for God?

3. What is the danger in staying stuck in the past?

4. Is there some old behavior that wasn't good for you that you find yourself going back to? What can you do to beat it once and for all?

5. Pray this. Father, you are the God of my destiny. I will trust you with my future, and I will not be afraid. Show me any area of my life that needs pruning and help me submit to the process. Amen.

Chapter 5

Jochebed-Trusting God with Your Sacrifice

Exodus 2:1-10

Why do we hold onto things so tightly? Closing our hands protects what is inside, but it also ensures that we can receive nothing else. Meet Jochebed, a pregnant Hebrew woman in a very difficult situation. In Exodus Chapter 1, we learn that the children of Israel are multiplying. It seems that the more they are oppressed, the more they grow. So, the king of Egypt goes to the midwives and instructs them to kill every male born to the Hebrew women.

Such is the mandate when Jochebed gives birth to her beautiful baby boy. She hides him for three months but knows that he cannot remain hidden forever. She takes him, places him into a basket, and puts him into the Nile River. She sends her daughter, Miriam, to watch the basket from afar. Miriam likely watches with anticipation and fear. What will become of her baby brother? Will he fall out of the basket and drown? Will a crocodile or alligator have him for breakfast? Will he cry so loudly that he is discovered and killed?

Miriam will actually have a front-row view of the Divine Providence of God. As the basket floats along in the reeds, Pharaoh's daughter notices the basket. She sends her maid to retrieve it and discovers a baby inside! A baby boy! Remember the law. Every Hebrew male child must be killed. You must also remember that God is a fact breaker. It is a fact that the male children were supposed to be killed, but it is a greater truth that God is sovereign. He can do whatever He wants to do.

In this case, there is a specific agenda for the life of that young baby, and God protects His plan! Miriam watches as they retrieve her brother, and she runs to Pharaoh's daughter, making a very strategic suggestion. "Shall I go and call a nurse for you from the Hebrew women, that she may nurse the child for you?" Exodus 2:7. Pharaoh's daughter agrees, which positions Jochebed as nurse to her very own baby boy. Isn't God strategic? Isn't His attention to detail absolutely amazing? Rather than having to bury her child, God provides a way for Jochebed to nurse her own baby and allow him to grow up in the house of the king.

It is difficult at times to release things and to let them go, but remember the story of Jochebed. As she entrusted something valuable into the hands of a loving God, He worked out the rest of the details.

We must learn to give our sacrifices to God because then, and only then, can He increase us and give us something good. We can trust Him as a Good Father and be comforted that He has great plans for our lives. Everything we sacrifice multiplies, and He gives us something greater than we ever could have dreamed.

God takes care of His children, and when He has a plan, He is faithful to perform it. Trust Him and refuse to hold tightly to things He is asking of you. Don't make Him pry it from your hands. Offer it freely. When you offer your everything to God, you will find that He creates something beautiful. He surprises you with something even better. God takes care of all the details. You never have to worry. Trust Him. You're too full to be empty!

Questions:

1. What is God asking you to sacrifice to him at this juncture in your life?

2. Why are you hesitating?

3. Can you think of a time in the past when you made a sacrifice that actually worked to your benefit?

4. What does our unwillingness to obey say about what we believe about God?

5. Pray this. Father, please let me hold nothing so tightly that it competes with your place in my life. Amen.

Chapter 6

Deborah-Leading as A Woman

Judges 4:1-14, 5:1-31

Many of you reading this book have been called to do something that is uncommon for your family, your gender, or station in life. Whenever we are called to do something spectacular for God, we are often confronted with whether we have the confidence to be who God has called us to be. In Judges 4, we are introduced to a very unique character in that of Deborah. Verse four tells us that Deborah was a prophetess, the wife of Lapidoth, who was judging Israel at that time. The children of Israel approached the tree under which she sat, and she rendered judgement for their issues and concerns.

One day, Deborah sends for Barak, and gives him a message from God, "The Lord, the God of Israel, commands you: 'Go, take with you ten thousand men of Naphtali and Zebulun and lead them up to Mount Tabor. I will lead Sisera, the commander of Jabin's army, with his chariots and his troops to the Kishon River and give him into your hands." Judges 4:7. Barak's response will likely surprise you. He tells Deborah, "If you go with me, I will go; but if you don't go with me, I won't go." Barak asks Deborah, a woman, to accompany him. In fact, he says even if God is sending me, I will not go if you do not go with me! That is some reputation. Deborah had obviously shown herself to be a trusted guide and resource for Barak to refuse to go to battle without her.

Deborah tells him that though she will agree to go with him, the glory for the victory will be given to a woman instead of him! Deborah rises to go with him, and as the enemy gathers for battle, Deborah delivers the word to go forward. "Go! This is the day the Lord has given

Sisera into your hands. Has not the Lord gone ahead of you?" Judges 4:14.

After the victory, Deborah sings a song to the Lord. She reminisces about the victory that comes to leaders who offer themselves to God. She remarks about how the highways were deserted and the travelers walked on the byways until her arrival. "Village life ceased until I, Deborah, arose as a mother in Israel. Judges 5:7. Deborah recognizes that it was when she arose and took her rightful position as leader, judge, and strategist that things shifted for her nation. Her voice and participation were an integral part of their shift to victory.

For a woman to be judge and prophetess was uncommon in that day, just as some of the things you are called to do. Perhaps you feel an unction to do something for which there is no existing prototype. Welcome to the club! You are a trailblazer. God is inviting you to go on a journey of faith with him. It has been said that if what you feel God is calling you to is not beyond your capability, it is likely not God. God rarely calls us to do anything that we could successfully do without him.

Being different establishes you as a pioneer and trailblazer, so don't shy away from it. Embrace your difference and the fact that God has called you to do something distinct and great. Being a woman who leads can at times be challenging, but always remember, you are built for this. When God puts his stamp of approval on you, no one or nothing can stop you. So, do not ever despise the fact that you are a woman. Beautiful. Strong. Feminine Bold. You are your Daddy's daughter! You are set up to win. You are too full to be empty!

Questions:

1. How easy is it for you to ask for advice?

2. How do you respond when someone gets credit for something that should go to you?

3. How can you defy a stereotype about you or your life?

4. If someone asks you for advice, how do you decide what to share with them?

5. Pray this. Father, help me to make righteous decisions for my life and always give advice and counsel that is based on your Word. May I never

despise that I am a woman. Use my life for your glory. Amen.

Chapter 7

Jael-Implementing a Winning Strategy

Judges 4:17-24

Many times, we are faced with a dilemma and we really just don't know what to do. It is in these moments that we must seek God for divine strategies and execution. You never know when you will be called to a divine moment that can change your destiny. All of the people we now know as celebrities were once regular people just like you and me. They lived normal lives in obscurity. Then suddenly, one day, opportunity met preparation, and just like that, they went from overlooked to overbooked. That is the power of a moment, of being prepared to seize a moment of opportunity with action.

In Judges 4, there is an intense war going on. Barack and his men pursue Sisera on chariots. All of the men are killed by the sword except Sisera. Somehow, miraculously, he escapes. He happens on the tent of Jael, and she welcomes him in. She welcomes him as she says, "Turn aside, my lord, turn aside to me; do not fear." I imagine that Sisera is relieved. He is running for his life and seemingly has found a safe place to rest. He follows her into the tent and lies down as she covers him with a blanket. He asks her for a drink of water, and she honors his request with a jug of milk. Before he fully relaxes, he has one last request. Sisera instructs Jael, "Stand at the door of the tent, and if any man comes and inquires of you, and says, 'Is there any man here?' You shall say, "No."

As Sisera falls into a deep sleep, Jael senses her moment. It is now or never. She grabs a tent peg, takes a hammer in her hand, tiptoes softly near where he is sleeping, and drives the peg into his temple! Just like that! Jael has taken the victory that was supposed to go to another--Barak, a man and the leader of his army. Now, just as Deborah prophesied, the victory of the army went to Jael—a wise woman who seized the power of a moment, stepped out in boldness and finished the job.

That's all it takes to be known as someone great. Perfect the gifts God has given you, remain sensitive to the moment, listen for instructions, and execute. Then, you too, can be victorious. Not everyone will ascend a huge platform or be seen on magazines or television, but everyone can make a choice that shifts destiny. Your decision or moment may come in the form of being the first one in your family to go to college, break a cycle of poverty, or live a sold-out life for God. Whatever the contribution, it will have a ripple effect that can change your life and the lives of others forever. If you can change your circle, your family, or your nation, you can make a mark on the world that will be remembered for generations to come. Seize the opportunity to take a risk and make a decision without being afraid. You are the solution to someone's problem. You are too full to be empty!

Questions:

1. When was the last time you did something that you were afraid to do?

2. What is a recurring issue in your family that you have a solution for?

3. What would you be doing now if you weren't afraid?

4. Take a few moments and talk with God about something you need Him to help you do. Ask Him to help you.

5. Repeat this sentence three times in a mirror. "I will not let fear stop me. I am a child of God." Amen.

Chapter 8

Delilah-Giving Way to A Spirit of Seduction

Judges 13:2-5; 16:1-20

Samson is a very familiar character, but perhaps you have never heard the miraculous story behind his birth. His mother and father were barren. They were childless. One day, his mother has a unique encounter.

> The Angel of the LORD appeared to the woman and said to her, 'Indeed now, you are barren and have borne no children, but you shall conceive and bear a son. Now therefore, please be careful not to drink wine or *similar* drink, and not to eat anything

unclean. For behold, you shall conceive and bear a son. And no razor shall come upon his head, for the child shall be a Nazirite to God from the womb; and he shall begin to deliver Israel out of the hand of the Philistines. Judges 13:3-5

This miraculous announcement has to bring to mind another birth and coming messenger from much later in the Bible. In fact, both men were prophesied as Israel's deliverers.

Samson's mother goes to her husband, Manoah, to report what occurred, and he immediately prays a prayer of deep wisdom, "O my Lord, please let the Man of God whom You sent come to us again and teach us what we shall do for the child who will be born." Judges 13:8. A couple of things to take note of here. First, it is obvious that Manoah has an appreciation and respect for God. He doesn't tell his wife that she is crazy or try to dispute her story. He simply accepts it and petitions God for instructions. What a tremendous blessing! If you are blessed to have a companion who seeks God for wisdom and instruction, you are above all women extremely blessed. If not, you can always petition God to change his heart. Always remember that "the heart of the king is in God's hands." Proverbs 21:1.

Often times we make the mistake of having an idea we think we heard from God, but moving forward without asking for clarity and instructions. He likely perceives that this birth has to be something special to get an angelic announcement, so he does not want to make a mistake. Seeking God for wisdom is paramount to being a woman who walks in confidence and power.

God answers his prayer, and the Angel appears again, confirming his earlier message. They offer a sacrifice to God, and the angel disappears. Verse 24 reveals the fulfillment of the promise, "So the woman bore a son and called his name Samson; and the child grew, and the Lord blessed him." God opens her womb, gives the child that was promised and blesses him.

Samson becomes a mighty warrior. He gets a wife, but she deceives him and is given to his best man! Much warfare happens in his life against the Philistines, and he becomes a proverbial thorn in their flesh. In Chapter 16, we meet Delilah, a woman he loves. The lords of the Philistines come to her and make an insidious request, "Entice him, and find out where his great strength lies, and by what means we may overpower him, that we may bind him to afflict him; and every one of us will give you eleven hundred pieces of silver." (16:5). Shocking, right? Who would think it plausible to get a woman to betray the man she is supposed to love? How could she agree to play a part in his demise?

This part of the story brings a powerful admonition. As women, we possess an innate ability to influence the men in our lives. Many women learn to use that ability in a way that is evil and wicked. These women soon learn that in bringing about his fall, they suffer also. Then there are the wise women. These are those who use their influence as an asset—women who add value, worth, and the contribution of insight and intuition. Which one are you? Do people remark about the value you bring to their lives or do they lament about the destruction you leave in your path? It's really something to consider.

Delilah will prove to be the latter as she agrees to the plan. She inquires of Samson, "Please tell me where your great strength lies, and with what you may be bound to afflict you." (16:8). This story always seems strange to me in that Samson doesn't seem to take her inquiry as strange. Perhaps he has heard the stories of God's covenant, so he has no concern about losing his strength. Maybe he is so mesmerized by her influence that his guard is down. We will never know what he was thinking, but he gives her a response, "If they bind me with seven fresh bowstrings, not yet dried, then I shall become weak and be like any other man." She relays the secret, gets the bowstrings from the Philistines, and binds him. When she cries, "Samson, the men are upon you," he easily breaks the cords, revealing that he had not told her the truth.

Three additional times, she questions Samson about the source of his strength, only to be duped. Delilah is frustrated that her plan is not working, so she resorts to seduction and manipulation, "How can you say, 'I love you,' when your heart is not with me? You have mocked me these three times and have not told me where your great strength lies." The Bible says she continues to pester him daily and presses him until "his soul was vexed to death!" Again, I've often wondered why Samson would continue to share his secret with Delilah when each time the Philistines came to attack him. Didn't he recognize the trend here? Couldn't he see that she was seeking to harm him?

The most obvious reason for this gullibility is pride. Samson always defeated everything that opposed him. He knew he was strong and fierce and feared by everyone. Perhaps that knowledge weakened his ability to discern that he was being set up for the kill. Just like many of us! How many times have you seen the warning signs, knew that something or someone was bad news, yet you kept going back to a thing that was destroying you?

Finally, she wears him down, and he tells her the truth. She calls for someone to cut his hair while he sleeps on her knees, then she begins to torment him. He awakens, clueless that his strength has left him and is bound, blinded, and taken to prison. All because he chose to sleep in the lap of someone who wanted to destroy him!

Women are given great beauty and charm, but both must be submitted to God. It's important that we recognize that even though women have been given unique influence through their beauty and ability to persuade, we do not want to be used to destroy someone we say we love, nor do we want to fall for the fallacy that our only value is our exterior. We are not to use our beauty and influence in a negative or seductive fashion. We do not want to be the vehicle that destroys someone that we say we love. Worse still, we do not want to be destroyed ourselves.

We must be very careful. There is a very fine line between being beautiful and thinking that beauty is all you have to offer. It is dangerous to use your beauty and charm for manipulation and seduction. That was not God's intention for the beauty and the unique traits and characteristics that he has given you as a woman. Don't ever seek to utilize the weaknesses of others against them and do not ever fall for the lie that all you have of worth and value is your body. You are loved. You are valued.

You are created with a specific purpose and destiny. Don't sell yourself short. You are too full to be empty!

Questions:

1. Have you ever used manipulation to get something you wanted? How did you feel afterwards?

2. How does God feel about controlling someone else's will?

3. In what ways does society support the belief that women should use their looks to get ahead?

4. How can you be attractive without being seductive?

5. What needs to change in your life so that people in your life see you as a safe place to expose their hearts?

6. Pray this. Father, help me to see my femininity and beauty as a gift to be celebrated and not as a tool for manipulation or exploitation. Amen.

C h a p t e r   9

Naomi-From Bitter to Blessed

Ruth 1:6-22

If anyone had cause to be broken and bitter, it was surely Naomi. The book of Ruth opens by introducing the reader to the family of Elimelech. He is married to Naomi and they have two sons, Mahlon and Chilion. They travel to Moab, and Elimelech dies. Suddenly Naomi is a widow with two sons. Both sons marry women from Moab and live there another ten years, then both sons die. The Bible says, "the woman survived her two sons and her husband." Ruth 1:5. Naomi has seemingly lost everything, but she will soon learn that she actually has something left.

Naomi decides that she will return to her homeland, Judah, so she tells her daughters-in-law, "Go, return each to her mother's house. The Lord deal kindly with you, as you have dealt with the dead and with me. The Lord grant that you may find rest, each in the house of her husband." Ruth 1:8-9. As they cry together, the women refuse to leave her. She questions why they should follow her since she can never provide husbands for them. She asks, "Why will you go with me? Are there still sons in my womb that they may be your husbands?" Ruth 1:11. Naomi sees no logical reason why the women should continue to stay with her as she has no hopes of ever providing husbands for them. Finally, Orpah concedes, but Ruth refuses. She promises to stay with her mother-in-law until the very end.

The two women travel to Bethlehem and all the people are excited to see Naomi. The women ask, "Is this Naomi?" Ruth 1:19. Naomi replies, "Do not call me Naomi; call me Mara, for the Almighty has dealt very bitterly with me. I went out full and the Lord has brought me home again empty. Why do you call me Nami since the Lord has testified against me, and the Almighty has afflicted me?"

Ruth 1:20-21. Can you identify with Naomi's story? Were you once successful or beautiful, too prosperous only to be left empty-handed? Have you lost something or someone very close to you? Perhaps you have been forced to bury a husband or child or someone that you loved dearly.

You must not make the mistake Naomi makes. While she grieves and bemoans her plight, she is missing one very obvious component to her story. She has not lost everything. She has Ruth, her daughter-in-law. So great was Ruth's love for Naomi that she refused to leave her alone. She chose not to return to her home country so she can accompany Naomi. That is true sacrifice and love.

Yet, how often do we fall into the same trap? We spend so much time and energy looking at what or who we've lost that we forget to celebrate the ones who stayed. The people you have in your corner are reason to celebrate. Even though Naomi sees herself as empty, she has something very valuable—someone who has vowed to be loyal to her and stay by her side at her weakest point!

As you read the next chapter, you will discover that God has even more surprises in store for Naomi through

Ruth, her special gift. Both of their lives will be blessed as the story unfolds. Naomi's story should serve to remind you not to count yourself out. Do not throw in the towel just yet. It truly is not over until the fat lady sings! Focus on what you still have, not what you've lost. God is a redeemer of time and things. You are too full to be empty!

Questions:

1. What are some things you've lost that you can't seem to rebound from?

2. How can Naomi's story be an encouragement to you?

3. When have you been so focused on the negative that you totally missed something positive in your life?

4. When was a time that you misjudged God's intentions?

5. Pray: Father, teach me to trust you even when everything seems to be falling apart. I know you have promised never to leave me forsaken. Help me to see the light through the darkness. Amen.

Chapter 10

Ruth-From Widow to Wealthy

Ruth 1:16-18; 4:10-22

Great success often follows our willingness to make sacrifices for others. When we are down or broken, our natural tendency is to invert all our energies, but the greatest blessings come from doing exactly the opposite. What we make happen for others, God makes happen for us. In the last chapter, we were introduced to a man, Elimelech, his wife, Naomi, and their two sons.

Naomi's husband and sons die, leaving her with her daughters-in-law. Grieving her losses, Naomi decides to return to her home country. Naomi discourages Ruth and

Orpah from following her. In fact, she is so bound by grief that she has lost hope in God's ability to provide for them. Orpah takes Naomi up on her offer and decides to return to her homeland. Ruth refuses, telling her,

> Entreat me not to leave you, or to turn back from following after you;
>
> For wherever you go, I will go; And wherever you lodge, I will lodge;
>
> Your people shall be my people, And your God, my God.
>
> Where you die, I will die, and there will I be buried.
>
> The Lord do so to me, and more also, If anything but death parts you and me. Ruth 1:16-17.

The women have no idea at the time, but they are both about to be blessed tremendously. Chapter Two introduces us to Naomi's relative. "There was a relative of Naomi's husband, a man of great wealth, of the family of Elimelech. His name is Boaz." Ruth 2:1. Umm. Looks like this might get interesting after all.

Ruth asks Naomi for permission to glean in the fields of someone who will show her favor, and Naomi agrees.

As Ruth gleans the field, the Bible tells us that she "happens" to be gleaning in the field of Boaz. Soon, Boaz notices her, and inquires who she is. The servant informs him that she had asked permission to gather from the fields and had only taken a small rest. Two small things to take note of here before we move forward. First, Ruth is not idle or lazy. She moves quickly to begin making provision for her and Naomi. This diligence positions her to be in the right place at the right time. Secondly, she made no assumptions and was not pushy or bossy. She sought permission to glean the fields and only rested for a short period. These details remind us that our hard work always pays off. As we put our hands to the plow, God begins working on our behalf.

Boaz immediately takes note and moves to bless her. "Then Boaz said to Ruth, 'You will listen, my daughter, will you not? Do not go to glean in another field, nor go from here, but stay close by my young women. Let your eyes be on the field which they reap, and go after them. Have I not commanded the young men not to touch you? And when you are thirsty, go to the vessels and drink from what the young men have drawn." Ruth 2:8-9. Ruth doesn't have to manipulate anyone or debase herself for favors. Boaz tells her she can glean in his field and instructs her to stay close to the young women in the field. He has given orders that the men are not to harass or touch her, and she is encouraged to drink from his vessels whenever she is thirsty. Look at God! He is Jehovah Jireh, the God of our provision.

Of course, Ruth wonders why Boaz has decided to favor her, so she asks him. His answer may shock you, but it simply evidences that we always reap what we sow. It doesn't always happen where or with whom we sowed, but we will reap nonetheless.

> And Boaz answered and said to her, "It has been fully reported to me, all that you have done for your mother-in-law since the death of your husband, and how you have left your father and your mother and the land of your birth, and have come to a people whom you did not know before. The Lord repay your work, and a full reward

be given you by the Lord God of Israel, under whose wings you have come for refuge." Ruth 2:11-12.

Ruth's sacrifice is being honored. Caring for her mother-in-law, has garnered favor for Ruth and Naomi. Boaz ends up inviting her to dinner and even tells the reapers to allow extra grain to fall for her so that she may recover it. Ruth is set up to receive double for her trouble!

When Ruth tells Naomi about her experience, Naomi reveals that Boaz is her relative. Ruth shares the instructions Boaz has given her for gleaning, and Naomi tells her it is good that she remains in Boaz's field. Then, she gives Ruth a plan that will secure her future. Naomi tells Ruth to wash herself, put on her best garment, and go to the threshing floor. When Boaz finishes eating and drinking, she instructs her to uncover his feet, lie down, and wait for instructions. Ruth follows Naomi's instructions, and when Boaz asks who she is at his feet, Ruth tells him that she is his maidservant who should be taken under his wing as a close relative.

Boaz is shocked by her request as he is an older man. He remarks that she has shown even more kindness by not going after younger men, whether poor or rich. He gives Ruth a guarantee that she will be taken care of, but there is a matter that must be addressed. He says, "Now it is true that I am a close relative; however, there is a relative closer than I. Stay this night, and in the morning, it shall be that if he will perform the duty of a close relative for you—good; let him do it. But if he does not want to perform the duty for you, then I will perform the duty for you, as the Lord lives!" Ruth 3:12-13. Boaz gives Ruth barley for Naomi as she returns home, and he tells everyone that no one is to know she was there. Boaz is proving to be an honorable man. This is a very important trait to have in a man who seeks to marry you. He should be a provider and always seek to protect your reputation.

Ruth returns to Naomi the next morning and recounts the events of the day. Naomi instructs Ruth to relax as she is certain Boaz will get the matter sorted quickly. Boaz calls a meeting with the relative, and the closer relative says he has no interest because taking Ruth will ruin his own inheritance. Boaz confirms the matter with his countrymen, and in Chapter 4 we learn that Ruth becomes his wife. They conceive a son, and the women pray a blessing over the child, "Blessed be the Lord, who has not left you this day without a close relative; and may his name be famous in Israel! And may he be to you a restorer of life and a nourisher of your old age; for your daughter-in-law, who loves you, who is better to you than seven sons, has borne him." Ruth 4:14-15. It should be noted that the child borne to Ruth was Obed, the father of Jesse, who was the father of King David. Because of Ruth's sacrifice ad faithfulness, her son became part of the lineage of Jesus Christ!

We never know exactly what God has in mind when He asks us to make a sacrifice, but we can be assured that He is up to something good. Even when it seems as if we have lost everything, God has a way of working things around. He comes on the scene to redeem us and show us that He is indeed the Giver of all gifts who does all things well. Don't lose hope. You are too full to be empty!

Questions:

1. What are you facing today that you believe can't be fixed?

2. Think about a time when something worked out differently than you planned. How was God at work behind the scenes?

3. In what ways has God given you beauty for ashes?

4. What have you sacrificed that actually ended up blessing your life?

5. Pray this. God, you are the God who makes all things new. Bring a miraculous turnaround in my life in the area of _____. I trust you. Amen.

Chapter 11

Hannah: Leveraging Prayer for a Miracle

1 Samuel 1:1-28; 21-11

Hannah's story begins in First Samuel. When we look at her introduction, we can immediately identify that she is empty. The Bible tells us that Hannah is married to a man named Elkanah. One of the problems is that she is not his only wife. Elkanah is also married to Peninnah. This signals that there is probably going to be a significant problem. Remember Sarai and Hagar. Two wives in a house, sharing one man just doesn't seem to be a recipe for peace and harmony.

Peninnah has birthed children. Hannah has not. She is barren. The Bible also reveals something very surprising, perhaps difficult to fathom. "The Lord had closed her womb." Wait! Read that again. The Lord closed her womb. There is no explanation. No reason. Just the fact. There have been no children because the Lord said, "no." So just in case we are confused about who creates life, who gives life, and who sustains mankind, the Bible sets the record straight. Even in Jeremiah, God says, "Before you were formed in your mother's womb, I knew you. Before you were born, I sanctified you; I ordained you a prophet to the nations." Jeremiah 1:5.

This verse alone silences the debate about conception. Even before a baby enters the world, it has a destiny and purpose. Hannah's closed womb isn't something she is responsible for. Invitro or modern-day technology would be of no use here. When God closes something, no one can open it.

When the time comes each year to sacrifice and worship, Elkanah gives offering portions to Peninnah and her sons and daughters. He gives a double portion to

Hannah because he loves her, but still, there is tension. In fact, the Bible says, "And her rival also provoked her severely, to make her miserable, because the Lord had closed her womb." 1 Samuel 1:6. There's some humanity showing here. Peninnah makes sure Hannah doesn't forget that she is able to give Elkanah something Hannah can't. Year after year, they go to make their annual sacrifice, and Peninnah provokes Hannah, making her so sad that she refuses to eat.

When Elkanah notices Hannah's depression, he asks, "Hannah, why do you weep? Why do you not eat? And why is your heart grieved? Am I not better to you than ten sons?" Sometimes, men just don't quite get it. He doesn't understand how Hannah feels. We can all identify with trying to express ourselves with our brother, dad, or husband. Communication can be challenging at times because we are wired very differently.

This year, though, Hannah decides to do something different with her pain. She cries out to God and makes a promise. "O Lord of hosts, if You will indeed look on the affliction of Your maidservant and remember me, and not forget Your maidservant, but will give Your maidservant a male child, then I will give him to the Lord all the days of his life, and no razor shall come upon his head." 1 Samuel 1:11.

This is no fly-by-night prayer. This a heartfelt cry of desperation. This is the kind of prayer that gets God's attention. Hannah has come to the end of herself. She is tired of feeling less than. She doesn't like feeling that she can't measure up and give her husband a child. Her frustration leads her to a positive step, though. She makes her case with the only one who can change her situation.

How about you? Do you find yourself complaining about your life? Do you spend your time frustrated because something just isn't working? Skip the line and go straight to the Father. He hears the cries of his children, and nothing is too hard for him. Jeremiah 32:27.

As she prays, Eli, the priest, notices her lips moving but doesn't hear her words. He thinks she is drunk, and rebukes her, "How long will you be drunk? Put your wine away from you!" 1 Samuel 1:14. Isn't it just like people to misjudge our pain?

Hannah could have "gone off" or asked him if he was crazy, but cooler heads prevail, and as we continue through the story, we will see that she will be glad she did. Hannah responds with respect and reverence. "No, my lord, I am a woman of sorrowful spirit. I have drunk neither wine nor intoxicating drink, but have poured out my soul before the Lord. Do not consider your maidservant a wicked woman, for out of the abundance of my complaint and grief I have spoken until now." 1 Samuel 1:15-16.

Hannah's response garners her favor and a blessing. Eli answers, "Go in peace, and the God of Israel grant your petition which you have asked of Him." 1 Samuel 1:17. Hannah asks for favor, and the Bible tells us that she goes away and eats, as she is no longer sad.

The next verse tells us that as they rose to return home, Elkanah knew his wife, and "the Lord remembered her." 1 Samuel 1:19. Well, that's all we need to know, right? Because when the Lord remembers you, everything is taken care of. It's a done deal. We clamor and work for the acknowledgement of men and women and try to achieve worldly status and fame, but there is no substitute for the Lord remembering you! When the Lord remembers you, you are guaranteed to get the best life has to offer. He always finishes what he starts.

Hannah bears a son, nurses him, and returns him to the temple to remain with Eli, just as she had promised. God kept his end of the bargain. Hannah kept hers. What about you? Have you made an idle promise to God in desperation that you have failed to keep? Are you honoring him with your life and using the talents and skills he has given you for his glory?

Hannah is honorable. She keeps her promise to God. She returns the child he has blessed her with back to him for his safekeeping and service. How about you? Are you sitting up at night worrying yourself to death over your wayward child? Have you promised to let God handle your children, but still find yourself taking them back from the altar as soon as you finish praying? God knows what we all need better than we ever could, and he has promised to take care of us. Don't worry and get anxiety and high blood pressure trying to control others. Give them to God and watch him work.

The pinnacle of Hannah's story is the beautiful prayer she prays to God in Chapter 2. I encourage you to take time to read it in its entirety. Hannah praises God and celebrates his faithfulness. She acknowledges that there is no one like God and that He alone weighs our actions. He guards the feet of the saints and thunders against His adversaries. It is He who gives strengths to kings and exalts the horn of His anointed. He is worthy of praise!

God is in control of everything. We would do well to trust Him with our lives and everything we are concerned about. He is faithful. Maybe you have had an abortion or miscarriage and think you can never conceive again. Talk to God about it. You don't have to cry yourself to sleep and figure out how to make things work. Cry out to him. He is waiting to hear from you. You're too full to be empty!

Questions:

1. **Do you trust God with everything that concerns you?**

2. Make a commitment to pray every time you are tempted to complain for the next three days.

3. What is something you have been worrying about lately?

4. Turn your concern into a prayer and pray it now.

Chapter 12

Abagail-A Wise Wife's Intervention

1 Samuel 25:2-35

Abigail is married to a very wealthy man named Nabal. In fact, he has three thousand sheep and goats. The Bible description of them stands in stark contrast. "And she was a woman of good understanding and beautiful appearance; but the man was harsh and evil in his doings." I Samuel 25:2.

At a certain time, Nabal is shearing the sheep in Carmel. David, the king, hears that Nabal is shearing his sheep and sends a blessing and a request that Nabal send him whatever comes to his hand to him. Remember, David is the king, so to make such a request would not be outlandish or unthinkable. Apparently, though, Nabal did not agree as is evidenced by his brazen response, "Who is David, and who is the son of Jesse? There are many servants nowadays who break away each one from his master. Shall I then take my bread and my water and my meat that I have killed for my shearers, and give it to men when I do not know where they are from?" 1 Samuel 25:10-11.

Probably not a wise move, huh? When David's men return with Nabal's response, David does not waste time. He tells the men to gird up their swords. He and 400 of his men prepare to take what he asked for! One of the men goes to share what is unfolding with Abigail, Nabal's wife. He recounts how David's men had been kind to them in the field and tells her that without intervention, they will face great harm. "Abigail acted quickly. "She took two hundred loaves of bread, two skins of wine, five dressed sheep, five seahs of roasted grain, a hundred cakes of raisins and two hundred cakes of pressed figs and loaded them on donkeys." 1 Samuel 25:18. She sends her servants ahead and rides toward David and his men.

Just as she reaches him, David tells his men that it was fruitless to provide protection for Nabal's men. He vows that he will not leave any men alive when they are done. Abigail immediately dismounts, falls on her face, and bows before David. She begs for forgiveness and tells him that the Lord will bless him and avenge him if he turns back and does not shed blood without cause.

David heeds her voice and tells her that she may go in peace. Abagail returns home assured that she has circumvented the death of the men. When she returns home, Nabal is hosting a fest, so she chooses to keep quiet. In the morning, once he has sobered up, she tells him what occurred. The Bible says that his heart became "like stone," and ten days later, the Lord struck him, and he died! 1Samuel 25:18.

When David hears the news, he celebrates that Abigail kept him from making the grave mistake of taking vengeance into his own hands. As a reward, David sends word to Abagail that he wishes to make her his wife! After using wisdom to avert great crisis, Abagail becomes wife to the king.

Perhaps you are married to a foolish or angry man or work for an angry boss. Maybe you are impulsive and make decisions from your emotions. Do not despair. Seek the God of all wisdom for a strategy to overcome the evil influences and help you turn the situation into something good. Abigail's quick thinking saved many lives and positioned her to be respected and recognized by the king. You never know how God will use you if you will simply trust Him. Scripture tells us that he uses the foolish things of the world to confound the wise. 1 Corinthians 1:27. Trust Him and ask Him for the answers you seek. You do not have to wander around blindly in the dark. The God of all flesh longs to help you. You are too full to be empty!

Questions:

1. **When was a time when you have been hotheaded and made a huge mistake?**

2. **How can you begin to practice allowing cooler heads to prevail?**

3. When did a hopeless situation end up turning out much different than you planned?

4. Pray: Father, help me put my emotions under the protection of your wisdom so I do not end up doing something I regret. I want to be sober and well-balanced, just as you commanded. I give my emotions to you. Teach me how to use them as a blessing, not a curse. Amen.

Chapter 13

Tamar-Living with Shame and Abuse

2 Samuel 13:1-20

Every decision we make has a ripple effect. Nothing we do only affects us. Everyone connected to our lives now and in the future will be impacted by the choices we make today. Sam Walton is no longer alive. In fact, he passed away in 1992. Yet, because he made a choice to start a small store of discounted merchandise in Bentonville, Arkansas, every person in his bloodline reaps the benefits. There are very few people on this planet who have not heard of Walmart.

We cannot readily accept the joy of knowing that good things flow to us from positive decisions without the sobering reality that negative choices have the same ability to impact us and those connected to our lives.

In Second Samuel 11, when other kings are at war, David is walking around on his rooftop. He sees a beautiful woman bathing, sends for her, and sleeps with her. When she sends word that she is pregnant, David finds himself in a quandary because she is married to a soldier in his army. He devises a scheme to get her husband to sleep with her. When that plan fails, he issues a directive that her husband be placed in the heat of battle so that he will be killed!

If you are unfamiliar with this Biblical narrative, you might have thought you were reading a script from a soap opera, but you aren't. Isn't it reassuring to know that nothing is new under the sun? Biblical characters faced many of the same issues we deal with today.

After her period of grieving, David takes the woman as his wife and she bears a son. The key to this story is in the final story of this chapter, "But the things that David had done displeased the Lord." 2 Samuel 11:27.

It is foolish to think that anything we do is ever really private. Even if no earthly person sees us or know what we are doing, we can be assured of one who does. God is omniscient. That means He knows all things. So even when you think you are getting away with something or escaping punishment, you must remember that the Bible promises we will reap what we sow.

In Chapter 12, the prophet Nathan comes to visit David. He shares a story about a rich man who takes advantage of a poor man, and David is enraged. He responds, "As surely as the Lord lives, the man who has done this shall surely die! And he shall restore fourfold to the lamb, because he did this thing and has no pity." 2 Samuel 12:5-6. I'm pretty sure David is not ready for Nathan's response when he replies, "You are the man!" As punishment, David learns that the sword will never leave his house, God will raise up adversity against him from within his own house, and his wives will be given to his neighbors to lie with in broad daylight!

This backdrop is important to know as we look into the story of Tamar because she is David's daughter. Whenever we are faced with any decision, we must remember that our children will confront the obstacles that we build with our poor decisions. Sin patterns travel through families until someone is bold enough to repent and do things differently.

In chapter 13, we are introduced to Tamar. She is described as beautiful, and we also learn that one of David's sons is madly in love with her. In fact, his lust for her is so extreme that it makes him physically sick. "Amnon was so distressed over his sister Tamar that he became sick, for she was a virgin. And it was improper for him to do anything to her." 2 Samuel 13:1. Amnon's friend, Jonadab, devises a scheme to get Tamar alone with him.

So Jonadab said to him, 'Lie down on your bed and pretend to be ill. And when your father comes to see you, say to him, 'Please let my sister Tamar come and give me food, and prepare the food in my sight, that I may see it and eat it from her hand.' Then Amnon lay down and pretended to be ill; and when the king came to see him, Amnon said to the king, "Please let Tamar my sister come and make a couple of cakes for me in my sight, that I may eat from her hand. 2 Samuel 13:5.

Amnon accepts the plan and begins its execution. He gets into bed, pretends to be ill, and asks David to send his daughter to tend to him, just as his friend suggested. Tamar comes to him, makes cakes for him, but when she offers them to him, he refuses. He tells her to make everyone else leave.

Once the coast is clear, Amnon calls for Tamar to bring the cakes into the bedroom to feed him. He grabs her hand and demands, "Come, lie with me, my sister." 1 Samuel 13:11. She pleads with him, "No, my brother, do not force me, for no such thing should be done in Israel. Do not do this disgraceful thing! And I, where could I take my shame? And as for you, you would be like one of the fools in Israel. Now therefore, please speak to the king; for he will not withhold me from you." 2 Samuel 13:12-13. Amnon has no concern for her honor or integrity. He is set on fulfilling his lust. Tamar is too weak to fight him off, so he rapes her.

The next line in the story is heartbreaking. "Then Amnon hated her exceedingly so that the hatred with which he hated her was greater than the love with which he had loved her. And Amnon said to her, "Arise, be gone!" 2 Samuel 13:15. Now that Amnon has deceived her, violated her, and taken her virginity against her will, Tamar becomes the object of his disdain! He orders her out of his sight. She begs him to allow her to stay to protect her honor, but he orders a servant to put her out. "And the servant put her out and bolted the door behind her."

Tamar tears her robe and covers her head with ashes as she weeps bitterly. When Absalom, their brother, comes to her, he asks if she has been violated by their brother and tells her to hold her peace. The Bible tells us that Tamar remained desolate in Absalom's house, David was very angry, and Absalom "spoke neither good nor bad to his brother for he hated him because he had forced their sister, Tamar." 2 Samuel 13:22. You can probably discern that this situation is far from over.

Bitter hearts seek a place for expression and Absalom's heart is no exception. After two full years pass, Absalom asks David and his men to accompany him and his sheepherders. When David refuses, Absalom asks if Amnon and the king's other sons may go. He gives his servants a command; when Amnon becomes merry with wine, they are to strike him dead! The servants obey and Amnon is killed at the command of his brother. Tamar's violation is avenged, but it has come at a very high cost! Nathan's prophecy over David's life is being fulfilled.

I sense that this story is causing some very powerful emotions to rise in you as you read this story. Perhaps you were violated as a child. Maybe you had your innocence violently stolen. Perhaps someone overpowered you on a date, or maybe you are in an abusive, loveless marriage, where marital relations are forced rather than consented to. Breathe. God wants to use this story to heal you. Now. Let Him. Take a break here and allow the healing to take place. You are too full to be empty!

Questions:

1. What painful memory did the story cause to surface?

2. How should you deal with it?

3. Is there someone who needs to hear your story?

4. Pray. Father, you know my story and you know the memories that need to be healed. Please come to me now and let's begin this process. I am ready. I know am created in Your image. I am too full of potential and your image to be broken. Help me heal. Amen.

Chapter 14

Michal-Blinded by Bitterness

I Samuel 18:20-21;2 Samuel 6:16-23

King Saul was very intimidated by David. He feared for his life, so he suggested that he would give David his oldest daughter, Merab, in exchange for fighting for him. His plan was not at all an innocent one. "For Saul thought, let my hand not be against him, but let the hand of the Philistines be against him" 1 Samuel 18:17. Saul hoped that David's demise would come at the hand of the Philistines rather than his.

Although Merab should've been given to David, Saul gives her to another man as his wife. Soon after, Saul learns that his younger daughter is in love with David, so he concocts another plan. So, Saul said, "I will give her to him, that she may be a snare to him, and that the hand of the Philistines may be against him. 1 Samuel 18:21.

Michal and David are married. One day David leaves for battle. He returns from a victory with the ark in a time of celebration. The Bible says that David dances before the Lord with all his might. As David enters the city in jubilation, something very bizarre happens. "Now as the ark of the Lord came into the City of David, Michal, Saul's daughter, looked through a window and saw King David leaping and whirling before the Lord; and she despised him in her heart." 2 Samuel 6:16. David's joy infuriates Michal. It actually makes Michal hate him! Where did this bitterness come from? What happened in her life to cause Michal to be unable to celebrate with her husband? We will never know.

As David blesses the people, he returns to bless his household. It is now that he comes face to face with the scorn and disdain of his wife. "And Michal the daughter of Saul came out to meet David, and said, "How glorious was the king of Israel today, uncovering himself today in the eyes of the maids of his servants, as one of the base fellows shamelessly uncovers himself!" 2 Samuel 6:20. Wow! Not only is David a valiant warrior, but he is also Michal's husband. To respond to him like this was not only disrespectful, but it could also have been dangerous. David's response seals the deal.

> So, David said to Michal, it was before the Lord, who chose me instead of your father and all his house, to appoint me ruler over the people of the Lord, over Israel. Therefore, I will play music before the Lord. And I will be even more undignified than this, and will be humble in my own sight. But as for the maidservants of whom you have spoken, by them I will be held in honor." 1 Samuel 6:21-22.

David reminds Michal how he ascended to popularity and that her father is currently only keeping the seat warm for him! To further incense her, he says, I will get even crazier than this as I celebrate all that God has done, and as a matter of fact, the handmaidens you referenced will receive the honor that could have been yours. Hmmm. How is that for serving someone a slice of humble pie!

Michal's love turned quickly to bitterness, and as a result, she lost the strength of her femininity. Chapter Six ends with a sobering sentence, "Therefore Michal the daughter of Saul had no children to the day of her death." 2 Samuel 6:23. Michal's bitterness caused a barrenness than defined the remainder of her life.

We would be wise to learn from Michal's mistake. We must guard our heart against pain and trauma so that we do not allow it to ferment in our heart. If we do not, we can become angry and bitter, and we become someone everyone seeks to avoid. Bitterness can cause us to alienate someone God sent to bless us, and we could end up unproductive and barren for the duration of our lives. Allow this story to shake you whenever you consider holding unforgiveness in your heart. If allowed to fester, it can destroy your life. Forgiveness protects your heart and makes you a magnet for people who will love you. Do not harbor pain and allow it to grow in your heart. You can't afford to be bitter. You are too full to be empty.

<u>Questions</u>:

1. Who do you need to forgive?

2. How is it affecting your heart and health?

3. What has not happened in your life that you think should have?

4. What will you do with your bitterness?

5. Pray: Father, help me bring all of my pain, heartache and frustration to you. I do not want to carry the cancer of unforgiveness in my heart. Today by an act of my will, I decide to release everyone who ever hurt me. Help me to heal. Amen.

Chapter 15

Jezebel-Obsessed with Control

1 Kings 16:31; 18:4;1 Kings 19:1-2;1 Kings 21:1-16; 2 Kings 9:30-37

In 1 Kings Chapter 16, we are introduced to Jezebel and learn that she is married to Ahab. In Chapter 18, we discover that Jezebel massacred the prophets of the Lord. In Chapter 19, Ahab tells Jezebel how Elijah humiliated and murdered the prophets of Baal. Jezebel sends Elijah a very detailed message, "So let the gods do to me, and more also, if I make not thy life as the life of one of them by tomorrow about this time." 1 Kings 19:2. In 1 Kings Chapter 21, we read about a man named Naboth who has a vineyard next to the palace of Ahab and Jezebel. Ahab wants it, so he asks Naboth to trade with him or sell the land. Naboth refuses to give his inheritance to Ahab, so Ahab is extremely upset. When he goes home, he lies on his bed and refuses to eat.

Just as with Elijah, Jezebel comes in to ask what ails her husband. When he explains what transpired with Naboth, she tells him to rise and eat. She assures him that he will get the vineyard he wants. Jezebel proceeds to concoct a nefarious scheme. She writes letters in Ahab's names, seals them and sends them to the elders. The letters instruct the elders to, "Proclaim a fast, and seat Naboth with high honor among the people; and seat two men, scoundrels, before him to bear witness against him, saying, 'You have blasphemed God and the king.' Then take him out, and stone him, that he may die." 1 Kings 21:9-10.

Can we say ruthless? The men and elders of the city carry out her instructions and Naboth is stoned to death, all because he refused to give or sell his own vineyard. We learn that Jezebel makes good on her promise, as verse 16 tells us, "Ahab got up and went down to take possession of the vineyard of Naboth the Jezreelite." Jezebel finishes what she starts, and she always tries to make good on her evil threats, even if it means people die.

Let us never forget that we have an all-seeing God. Even when we think that we have gotten away with things, even when no one seems to know, we can be assured that God is always aware of everything we have done. The Lord comes to Elijah and tells him to go meet with Ahab just he has begun taking possession on Naboth's vineyard. Elijah asks Ahab what he has done then he renders God's impending judgement, "In the place where dogs licked up Naboth's blood, dogs will lick up your blood—yes, yours!" 1 Kings 21:19. You might be thinking, but it was Jezebel's idea. You're right, and God will not be mocked. Elijah has a word for her too. "And concerning Jezebel, the Lord also spoke, saying, 'The dogs shall eat Jezebel by the wall of Jezreel.' The dogs shall eat whoever belongs to Ahab and dies in the city, and the birds of the air shall eat whoever dies in the field." 1 Kings 21:23-24. Not a message you'd be eager to receive, is it?

When we make wicked decisions, there are always consequences. When Jehu comes to Jezreel, Jezebel learns of it. "She put paint of her eyes and adorned her head, and looked through a window." 2 Kings 9:30. She asks Jehu if he has come in peace, then Jehu goes to work, "And he looks up at the window and questions, "Who is on my side? Who? So, two or three eunuchs looked out at him. Then he said, 'Throw her down.' So, they threw her down, and some of her blood spattered on the wall and on the horses; and he trampled her underfoot." 2 Kings 9:33. Finally, the wrath of Jezebel has come to dramatic end.

Now that Jehu has finished the job, he goes in to eat and drink. He tells the eunuchs, "Go now, see to this accursed woman, and bury her, for she was a king's daughter." 2 Kings 9:34. Unfortunately, she cannot receive a proper burial because "when they went to bury her, they found no more of her than the skull and the feet and the palms of her hands. 2 Kings 9:35. What a horrible way to die! Devoured by dogs.

Jezebel was married to a passive man who allowed her bloodthirsty lust for power to go unchecked. Ahab actually took advantage of her ambition as she orchestrated many of his dirty deeds for him. Now they both came to an embarrassing, violent end. We would do well to remember the lesson of Jezebel when we move and function in our modern society. Many in culture will push you to assert yourself. They may urge you to leverage your femininity for position and power. They might even encourage you to rely on vindictiveness and competition to succeed. Many women fall into the trap as they view other women as enemies, and they use manipulation to get what they want. Whenever you are tempted to cause someone else's demise so you can succeed, remember Jezebel. It does not end well. Trust God to bless you and give you the things you need. You don't have to destroy others. Resolve not to be used as a tool by the devil. You are too full to be empty!

Questions:

1. **When was the last time you tried to manipulate or control a situation?**

2. **Do you need to apologize to someone for causing their downfall?**

3. Write down three ways that God has come through for you to use as reminders the next time you are struggling.

4. Pray: Father, help me to be an instrument of blessing not cursing. I want to be used to help others not hurt them. Help me to be motivated to do my best without being vindictive or destructive. Amen.

Chapter 16

Esther-Born for a Time Such as This

Esther 1-10

Have you ever been separated from home for any period of time? Stripped from everything familiar and sold into a life, not of your choosing? This is the story of Hadassah, better known as Esther. She is an orphan who is living with her cousin, Mordecai, when her life is suddenly turned upside down.

Because of the brazen disrespect of Queen Vashti, the king banishes her and begins a search for a new queen. Esther did not lobby for the position or long to leave her life to go to the palace. She is actually summoned and chosen to appear by God's providential hand.

Esther Chapter 2:8 tells us that the eunuch, Hegai is the custodian of women. He gathers all the women and Esther was taken into is custody. Verse nine tells us something very important. "Now the young woman pleased him, and she obtained his favor; so, he readily gave beauty preparations to her, besides her allowance." Hegai makes sure that Esther has everything she needs and even gives her the inside scoop about the king. We will soon discover that this favor will be on Esther's life throughout the book. Esther 2:17 tells us, "Esther obtained favor in the sight of all who saw her." Though God's name is never mentioned in this book, it is clear that His hand is at work. Of all the virgins sent to be chosen by the king, Esther receives the favor of God.

For one full year, Esther is trained, bathed, and prepared for her "opportunity." Each woman had one night with the king. If she is not chosen, she would leave the chambers rejected, yet used in whatever way the king saw fit. As the story folds, we can quickly discern that

Esther is no regular young woman. Though she does not know it, she has been uniquely chosen to change the entire destiny of her people. Esther has a date with purpose. She will be called to risk her life to save the life of many generations to come.

Finally, it is Esther's turn with the King Ahasuerus. We all hold our breath as we wait to learn her fate. "The king loved Esther more than all the other women, and she obtained grace and favor in his sight more than all the virgins; so, he set the royal crown upon her head and made her queen instead of Vashti." Esther 2:17. Esther is chosen by the King as his queen.

Beyond the king's court, Mordecai waits patiently to hear the outcome. As he goes about his business, his confidence and commitment to God earn him the hatred of Haman, the king's right-hand man. Thirsty for revenge, Haman gets to the king to agree to the extermination of the Jews, which are Esther's people.

When Mordecai learns of the plan, he covers himself with sackcloth and ashes and mourns at the gates. Esther sends word to him to end his mourning, but he does not relent. Finally, Esther seeks to discover the cause. When Mordecai reveals Haman's evil plot, he also tells Esther that it is her responsibility to intervene. Hearing that Esther was asked to speak to her husband in American culture seems like no big deal. But remember, her husband is the king. There were very strict rules about approaching the king without being summoned. To do so could mean death!

To ensure that Esther does not neglect her responsibility to her people, Mordecai reminds her that she too is one of them. If she refuses, God will certainly bring deliverance some other way, but she has been positioned as the queen by God to intercede for her people. She has attained a position of authority not only for herself, but so that she can stop the genocide. Esther agrees, but tells Mordecai to call a three-day fast for the people. At the end of the three days, she will approach the king. Her exact words are, "If I perish, I perish!"

At the end of fast, Esther goes before the king. As she approaches the king, he holds out his scepter to her, granting access to his throne. "And the king said to her,

'What do you wish, Queen Esther? What is your request? It shall be given to you—up to half the kingdom!" Esther 5:3. Esther asks the King Ahasuerus to come to a banquet she has prepared for him and to also invite Haman. Note something very important here. Esther doesn't go to the king demanding anything even though he is her husband. She respects his position as king and tells him that she wants to honor him with a banquet. Remember this important lesson. Honor opens doors of favor. There is nothing money can buy that favor and honor can't get for you. Paradoxically, dishonor can cause you to miss opportunities and cause people to reject you.

The King Ahasuerus and Haman come to the banquet and Esther decides to keep us all in suspense. Rather than make her request, she actually requests the king and Haman's presence at another banquet. As Haman exits, he encounters Mordecai at the gate and Mordecai refuses to pay homage to him. He is so angered that he tells his wife that despite being honored, he cannot be happy as long as Mordecai is sitting at the gate! His friends tell him to prepare gallows to hang him and asked the king to hang him there.

The next day when Esther, King Ahasuerus, and Haman convene at the banquet, the king asks Esther for her request. She tells him that her people are about to be killed. When the king inquires as to who would orchestrate such a tragedy, Esther tells him, "The adversary and enemy is this wicked Haman!" Esther 7:6 Can you imagine Haman's face? He was all set be honored and exalted only to have his plot against the Jews exposed!

The king goes into his garden in anger, and as he exits, Haman begins begging Esther for his life. "When the king returned from the palace garden to the place of the banquet of wine, Haman had fallen across the couch where Esther was. Then the king says, "Will he also assault the queen while I am in the house?" Esther 7:8. As punishment, Haman is hung on the gallows he prepared for Mordecai. What a turn of events!

Esther receives permission for the Jews to defend themselves, and Mordecai receives the honor that Haman thought he had reserved for himself. There are a few lessons we can learn from the story of Esther.

First, God's timing is perfect. You may think he has forgotten you, but you are never forgotten. God is always working all things together for good for those who are the called according to his purpose. Romans 8:28.

Second, you have a specific destiny that is ordained to change the world. There are no accidents in God. You, like Esther, are born for such a time as this to change and shift seasons, communities, even your very own family.

Third, God values humility. The Bible tells us that those who humble themselves will be given grace, and those who are proud will be resisted. James 4:8. If there is one person you cannot afford to resist you, that person is God.

Last, God is jealous over his children, and He will go to great lengths to protect the investment he has made in us. This should reassure you whenever you feel afraid or question what will happen next in your life. If you have accepted Jesus Christ as your personal Savior, you belong to God. He is committed to you and determined to bless your life. Don't doubt His heart toward you. What He begins, he is faithful to perform to completion. Do not grow weary in well doing. You are too full to be empty!

Questions:

1. When was a time you felt overlooked or forgotten?

2. How does the story of Esther encourage you?

3. Why is it best to let God take care of our enemies?

4. Pray: Thank you for favor. I thank you that I can trust that even when I cannot see or sense what you are doing. You are always at work. Help me rely on your divine protection over my life. You are a good Father, and I know you will take care of me.

Chapter 17

Leah- Surviving A Loveless Marriage

Genesis 29:15-30

When we are introduced to Leah, it is not with the most complimentary description. "Now Laban had two daughters: the name of the elder was Leah, and the name of the younger was Rachel. Leah's eyes were delicate, but Rachel was beautiful of form and appearance." Genesis 29:16-17. The New King James version uses a nicer form of the word than some of the other versions of the Bible. The New Living Translation describes her eyes as having no sparkle, and the Amplified version calls her eyes "weak."

Some theologians have said this means she was cross-eyed. I'm not completely sure, but to have your sister described as beautiful in form and appearance and have yourself described as having weak eyes can't be good.

After the Bible describes the sisters, we learn that Jacob is in love with Rachel. So much in love that he agrees to work for his uncle, Laban for seven years to have her. Laban agrees, and the seven years of working "seemed only a few days to him because of the love he had for her." Wow! To be loved like this must've made Rachel feel special, validated, and honored.

Finally, the seven years are up, and Jacob comes to Laban to claim his wife. Then Jacob said to Laban, "Give me my wife, for my days are fulfilled, that I may go in to her." Genesis 29:21. Laban gathers everyone and prepares a feast. But Laban has a trick in mind. "Now it came to pass in the evening, that he took Leah his daughter and brought her to Jacob; and he went in to her." Genesis 29:23. Wait! What? Laban sent in the wrong daughter. He had Jacob work for seven years for him only to renege on his promise! That's not fair. Well, you kinda have to know a little background about Jacob for this trickery to make sense. Read Genesis Chapter 27 to get up to speed on Jacob and how this situation is part of the fulfilment of sowing and reaping.

I must admit that each time I've read this story, I have wondered how it is that a man, who is supposedly so in love with a woman, sleeps with her sister and doesn't see or notice the difference. Let's get back to the story. "So, it came to pass in the morning, that behold, it was Leah. And he (Jacob) said to Laban, "What is this you have done to me? Was it not for Rachel that I served you? Why then have you deceived me?" Genesis 29:25. Prepare yourself for Laban's answer. It might shock you. He doesn't apologize. He doesn't say he got it wrong. "And Laban said, 'It must not be done so in our country, to give the younger before the firstborn. Fulfill her week, and we will give you this one also for the service which you will serve with me still another seven years." Genesis 29: 26-27. Basically, Laban says, Well, I could never give you the younger daughter to be married first, so if you really want Rachel, you will just have to work seven more years!

Jacob must've been really smitten because he agrees to work an additional seven years. After the seven years, he receives Rachel as his wife. Then Jacob also went in to Rachel, and he also loved Rachel more than Leah. Genesis 29:30.

Imagine being Leah. Your husband never chose you. He never wanted you. He chose and really desired your sister. But your father gave you to him instead. There's no celebration, no love, no honeymoon because your husband gets back to work for the woman he really wants. The woman who happens to be your sister. Imagine the pain, the rejection, the hopelessness Leah faces on a daily basis.

Perhaps Leah's life is a mirror of yours. Maybe you are married or in a relationship with a man who doesn't really want or desire you. Maybe you are the other woman, desperately waiting for a man to leave the woman he maintains he doesn't even love. It's time to face the truth and begin to deal with the pain and trauma. Otherwise, you may explode, or worse still, you may implode.

Even in our most difficult circumstances, we must never forget that God sees us. He longs to redeem us and give us beauty for ashes. He promises to work all things together for good for those who love Him. Stand on this promise and it will get you through some very difficult days.

God is committed to you, more than any man could ever be. He is your Father and even though challenges and difficulties come to our lives, he is faithful. We need only come to Him and confess our need of Him to be heard. The Bible tells us, "When the Lord saw that Leah was unloved, He opened her womb; but Rachel was barren." Genesis 29:31. God brings fruitfulness in a barren situation. Leah is able to give her husband children while Rachel cannot.

Leah's names for each of her sons reveal her heartache and pain and her hope that one day Jacob will love her too. Her first son Reuben means, "The Lord has surely looked on my affliction. Now therefore, my husband will love me." Genesis 29:32. Her second son Simeon means, "Because the Lord has heard that I am unloved, He has therefore given me this son also." Genesis 29:33. For her son Levi, "Now this time my husband will become attached to me, because I have borne him three sons." Genesis 29:34. Then, she had Judah who she names, "Now I will praise the Lord." When God closes her womb, she gives her maid to Jacob so that she can continue to conceive with Him. Later, God opens her womb again, and she has other children, but we never read that Jacob loved her. She gave him children, apparently performed as a wife, but she is never loved by him.

Leah's life is an example to remind us that life does not always hand us perfection. Sometimes we are dealt a difficult hand that is not at all our own doing. Often, we are forced to deal with and stomach an undesirable situation. Do not despair. You are not without hope. God will remember you if you just hold on to his promises. He has promised never to leave nor forsake you, even though earthly people may let you down. Hold on to your faith and persevere. Do not give up. You are too full to be empty!

Questions:

1. **What difficulty have you prayed to be released from that won't go away?**

2. **When have you felt forgotten or forsaken?**

3. What coping mechanisms have you put in place to deal with your pain and disappointment?

4. How can you begin to trust God to rescue you and give you peace in the meantime?

5. Pray. Father, everything in my life is not perfect. Many times, I may feel like there is no one who is in my corner or who really gets me. Help me to lean on you and trust in your name to deliver me and be my strong tower. Remind me that only when I come to you am I safe. Amen.

Chapter 18

Daughters of Zelophehad-
Using Your Voice for Justice

Numbers 36:1-13; 27:1-11

I want to be completely honest with you. The first time I read the Bible through, I had a sit-down with God. As I read the Old Testament, I begin to feel a little perturbed. I couldn't understand why God allowed women to endure so much. I saw women being passed around like property, used for their bodies, raped, and abused. It was if they had no value or voice. I suddenly blurted out, "God, do you even like women?" I kinda leaned to the side, expecting a lightning bolt and a deep thunderous voice to shout me down from Heaven. Instead, I was led to this story about the daughters of Zelophehad.

Then came the daughters of Zelophehad . . . . Mahlah, Noah, Hoglah, Milcah, and Tirzah. And they stood before Moses, before Eleazar the priest, and before the leaders and all the congregation, by the doorway of the tabernacle of meeting, saying: 'Our father died in the wilderness; but he was not in the company of those who gathered together against the Lord, in company with Korah, but he died in his own sin; and he had no sons. Why should the name of our father be removed from among his family because he had no son? Give us a possession among our father's brothers.' So, Moses brought their case before the Lord. Numbers 27:1-5.

Sometimes it feels unfair to be a woman. Women carry babies. Women are often paid less, and in many places, women have no voice and are the object of abuse. These daughters were the only ones left in their immediate family. There were no sons, so their family portion was about to be divvied up to others. The daughters come together and question the fairness of the allocation. They approach Moses in confidence because, inherently, they know that they should not be denied inheritance just because they are women. In wisdom, Moses takes the case before God.

> And the Lord spoke to Moses, saying, 'The daughters of Zelophehad speak what is right; you shall surely give them a possession of inheritance among their father's brothers, and cause the inheritance of their father to pass to them. And you shall speak to the children of Israel, saying: 'If a man dies and has no son, then you shall cause his inheritance to pass to his daughter. If he has no daughter, then you shall give his inheritance to his brothers. If he has no brothers, then you shall give his inheritance to his father's brothers.' And if his father has no brothers, then you shall give his inheritance to the relative closest to him in his family, and he shall possess it.' And it shall be to

the children of Israel a statute of judgment, just as the Lord commanded Moses.

Because of their courage to question being stripped of their inheritance, God established a new system. The daughters of Zelophehad remained heirs instead of being disinherited. The revelation from this story teaches us a few important things. First, God does love women. His heart has always been toward us and that has not changed. Second, we must be bold and courageous. If the daughters had remained silent, they would have lost their inheritance. Do not stand while your family is shaken or broken apart. Raise your voice and cry out to God for deliverance and see Him move on your behalf.

Never doubt that God loves you. He is forever committed to your health, your deliverance, and your healing. He sent His Son to die for your sins so that you could be restored to relationship with him. An incredible price was paid for your salvation. It is a sin to settle for any less. Fight the good fight of faith. War with the words that God has spoken over your life. His plans for you have not changed. Take heart, Daughter! You are too full to be empty!

Questions:

1. Have you lost something very valuable to you?

2. If you have not stood up for yourself when you should have, do you know why?

3. What things has the devil stolen that you want God to help you take back?

4. Pray. Father, for far too long I have allowed the enemy of my soul to intimidate me. I know you love me, and you purchased my wholeness with the blood of Jesus. Help me to rely on you. Help me to lift my voice and declare that everything you purposed for my life will be mine. I want to live the victorious life you purchased for me. I ask now for your help and I know you will hear me. Amen.

Chapter 19

The Shunammite Woman- Blessed Through Sacrifice

2 Kings 4:8-37; 2 Kings 8:1-6

Are there things in your life that you have resolved will always stay the way they are now? Is there something you really want but you've convinced yourself that you will have to live without it? The story of the Shunammite woman is for you. She was content living her life until an encounter changed her life forever. "Now it happened one day that Elisha went to Shunem, where there was a notable woman, and she persuaded him to eat some food. So it was, as often as he passed by, he would turn in there to eat some food." 2 Kings 4:8. We learn two important things about this woman from her early introduction. She is notable and she is generous. To be known and respected are not synonymous. There are many people who are popular, but some are considered infamous rather than famous.

Second, she gives food to the prophet and makes sure that she offers provisions whenever he comes through her town. She doesn't stop there, though. "And she said to her husband, 'Look now, I know that this is a holy man of God, who passes by us regularly. Please, let us make a small upper room on the wall; and let us put a bed for him there, and a table and a chair and a lampstand; so, it will be, whenever he comes to us, he can turn in there." 2 Kings 4:9-10. She goes a step further by telling her husband that they should prepare a guest room for him, so Elisha can remain comfortable whenever he comes around. If you are a gracious host or someone who loves to show honor, this story will encourage you to realize that you are setting yourself up to be blessed. The Kingdom of God functions on the principle of honor. Those who practice it can access everything they need.

One day, when Elisha and his servant, Gehazi are there, Elisha tells him to call the Shunammite woman to him. He tells him to ask her how he can reward her faithfulness. He offers to speak to the king or commander on her behalf, but she said that isn't necessary. So, Elisha asks Gehazi if he has a suggestion. Gehazi answers, 'Actually, she has no son, and her husband is old.' So, he said, 'Call her.' When he had called her, she stood in the doorway. Then he said, "About this time next year you shall embrace a son." 2 Kings 4:14-15.

The prophecy is so astonishing, so unexpected, that the woman does not believe it is true. And she said, "No, my lord. Man of God, do not lie to your maidservant!" 2 Kings 4:16. She has likely gotten used to being childless, so she has no expectation that her condition will ever change. But God has other plans. She has taken care of God's prophet, now she receives a prophet's reward. Matthew 10:41. Verse seventeen tells us that the woman conceives and bears a son, just as Elisha said.

The child grows, and one day, he goes out to the field with his father. He begins crying about his head, so his father tells a servant to take him to his mother. The Shunammite woman holds him in her lap until noon, then he dies! Watch her behavior closely to learn how to handle a crisis. "And she went up and laid him on the bed of the man of God, shut the door upon him, and went out. Then she called to her husband and said, 'Please send me one of the young men and one of the donkeys, that I may run to the man of God and come back." 2 Kings 4:21-22. She doesn't scream loudly and blame God for tricking her. She doesn't bemoan the tragic turn of events. She jumps into action.

When Elisha sees her coming, he sends Gehazi to meet her and asks if everything is okay. "And she answered, "It is well." When she reaches Elisha, she grabs him by the feet in her distress. Elisha sends Gehazi ahead with his staff and tells him to lay it on the face of the child. The woman refuses to leave without Elisha, so she and Elisha follow behind. As they travel, they meet Gehazi coming toward them, saying, "The child has not awakened." 2 Kings 4:31. Suddenly, a miracle begins to take shape,

> When Elisha came into the house, there was the child, lying dead on his bed. He went in therefore, shut the door behind the two of them, and prayed to the Lord. And he went up and lay on the child, and put his mouth on his mouth, his eyes on his eyes, and his hands on his hands; and he stretched himself out on the child, and the flesh of the child became warm. He returned and walked back and forth in the house, and again went up and stretched himself out on him; then the child sneezed seven times, and the child opened his eyes. 2 Kings 4:32-35.

Elisha tells his servant to call the woman, and she comes into the room to find her son alive! Later, Elisha instructs her to go to the land of the Philistines for seven years to avoid a famine. She obeys, and when she returns, she goes to make an appeal to the king. Gehazi tells the king about the miracle Elisha performed on her son. "So, the king appointed a certain officer for her, saying,

"Restore all that was hers, and all the proceeds of the field from the day that she left the land until now." 2 Kings 8:6. The favor of sacrifice and honor continues to follow her as her son is raised from the dead and all that she lost is restored!

This is the same thing that God desires to do for you if you will be hospitable, trust God, and show honor. Just as God favored the Shunammite woman, He will favor you. In fact, he already has. In this very moment, you are sitting in the middle of God's story for your life. It may not look like what you'd expect, but just remember everything can change in one moment! God is the God of miracles! He is the one who makes all things new. He is the restorer of your soul. God has not forgotten you. You are on His mind. Keep pushing! You are too full to be empty!

Questions:

1. **When was the last time you helped someone and expected nothing in return?**

2. **What have you given up on that you are sensing just needs a little persistence?**

3. What does the fact that Elisha clearing the room teach us about getting our prayers answered?

4. How can you use prayer to build your faith?

5. Pray about an area of your life where you feel like giving up.

Chapter 20

Rahab: From Harlot to Savior's Bloodline

Joshua 2:1-21; Hebrews 11:31; James 2:25

Sometimes we fear that our past is so soiled that God can never redeem us. Nothing could be further from the truth. The Bible tells us that there is none righteous, no not one. Romans 3:10. We are all in need of the forgiveness of the Father. We all need his saving grace. Without it, we are doomed to fail. This is why judging people's stories can be extremely dangerous. They could simply be in the middle of a story when you have decided that it is the end. God

127

has a way of making something beautiful from even the most dreadful sinner. Just ask Rahab.

The story of Rahab plays out in Joshua Chapter 2. Joshua sends to men to spy out the land they plan to take, especially Jericho. The Bible tells us that as they went, they came to the house of a harlot named Rahab. Just in case you wonder what a harlot is, a woman who was a harlot would be the modern prostitute or whore.

Word travels to the king that men have come to stake out the city and have gone to Rahab's house. The king of Jericho sends word to Rahab, saying, "Bring out the men who have come to you, who have entered your house, for they have come to search out all the country." Joshua 2:3. Word sure travels fast, right? She takes the men and hides them. Then she tells the king,

> Yes, the men came to me, but I did not know where they were from. And it happened as the gate was being shut, when it was dark, that the men went out. Where the men went, I do not know; pursue them quickly, for you may overtake them." (But she had brought them up to the roof and hidden them

128

with the stalks of flax, which she had laid in order on the roof.) Then the men pursued them by the road to the Jordan, to the fords. And as soon as those who pursued them had gone out, they shut the gate.

Once the coast is clear, she goes up to the roof and tells the men that everyone is afraid of them. The people in Jericho have heard how God had taken care of them and defeated their enemies, so they know they cannot defeat them.

Rahab uses this opportunity to ask for a favor," Now therefore, I beg you, swear to me by the Lord, since I have shown you kindness, that you also will show kindness to my father's house, and give me a true token, and spare my father, my mother, my brothers, my sisters, and all that they have, and deliver our lives from death." Joshua 2:12-13. Rahab is no dummy. She knows the defeat of Jericho is a foregone conclusion, but that doesn't mean that she and her family have to be obliterated too.

The men promise to take care of her family if she keeps their plan and visit secret, so she lets them down by a rope through a window. Before they leave, she gives them further instructions. "And she said to them, "Get to the mountain, lest the pursuers meet you. Hide there three days, until the pursuers have returned. Afterward you may go your way." Joshua 2:16. The men also have instructions for Rahab in order to secure her family's safety.

So, the men said to her, We will be blameless of this oath of yours which you have made us swear, unless, when we come into the land, you bind this line of scarlet cord in the window through which you let us down, and unless you bring your father, your mother, your brothers, and all your father's household to your own home. So, it shall be that whoever goes outside the doors of your house into the street, his blood shall be on his own head, and we will be guiltless. And whoever is with you in the house, his blood shall be on our head if a hand is laid on him. And if you tell this business of ours, then we will be free from your oath which you made us swear. Joshua 2:17-20.

As they leave, Rahab binds the scarlet cord in the window. When they return to defeat the city in Chapter 6, Rahab and her family are spared just as the spies promised.

Rahab and her family are spared from death, despite the fact that she had lived a sordid past. In fact, Rahab is in the lineage of Jesus! Whenever you think you are too dirty, too broken, or too messy for God, remember Rahab. She was used in the story of victory for God's people, and she is in the bloodline of our Savior. If you are willing, God will use you too. He will weave a beautiful tapestry out of your story and even use the events you never thought could be good for anything. God is Creator and He is masterful at creating beauty. Just look at you. Never again say you are not good enough. Never doubt the power of transformation in the hands of your Father. He loves you. You are a pearl of great price. You are the 1 He would leave the 99 for. You are the reason why Jesus came. Open your heart to Him and let Him in. You are too full to be empty!

Questions:

1. What are the negative issues surrounding your family reputation?

2. Pray to God to clear the generations that follow you beginning with you.

3. What part of your story are you most embarrassed of? Address any area of your personal life that brings you shame in prayer.

4. Ask God how He wants to use it for His glory.

5. Is there someone in your life that you have given up on? Contact them this week and prayer together.

6. Father, I thank you that you have promised if we confess our sins, you are faithful to forgive them. I confess that I need you and I ask you to forgive me of my sins. You are the God of new beginnings. Thank you for never giving up on me. I am grateful that your mercies are new every morning. Help me to fulfill my destiny in you and redeem my story for your glory. Amen.

Conclusion

Women are loved and created by God. We are innately crafted with life-giving potential, and we are creators and birthers of promise. You must never forget that. Even when life knocks you down or threatens to detour your destiny. If there is one thing we have learned through the stories of these women, it is this, Our God is faithful. He is not blind or deaf to our problems or plight and He always finds a way to bless us.

Writing this book is a labor of love for me that has been delayed and deterred for more than two years. I pray that you were blessed, inspired, and encouraged to think bigger, dream with passion, and determine not to let anything stop you from fulfilling your destiny.

There are many women in the Old Testament that I did not get a chance to cover here. Volume 2 will be women from the New Testament, so I encourage you to read the entire Biblical account of the women here and also to check out some notable women I did not explore like Miriam, Gomer, Rachel, Rebekah, Bathsheba, Dinah, the Shulamite woman, Jephthah's daughter, and everyone's favorite, the woman of Proverbs 31.

You come from a lineage of strong, enduring, and blessed women who pushed, persevered, and prayed their way through to victory. Truth be told, your story could be written here as a testament to God's faithfulness, mercy, and love. Maybe you will be inspired to write, or at least share your own story with the world, or perhaps a young woman who would be inspired to keep going.

You owe it to the world to be all that God created you to be. Jesus shed his blood for it. And God created a purpose just for you! No matter how you may feel. Regardless of whether you think or believe you have something to offer the world, YOU DO! God has invested all of Himself into you so that you could reach your potential and be more than you've ever dreamed. He would not have invested so much in you if you weren't a big deal. So, remember that! Walk in that! Live in that!

Manifest His reality for your life! You are TOO FULL to be empty!

If you have never received Jesus Christ as your Lord and Savior, now is your chance. Remember you don't have to be good, perfect, or ready. You just need to confess your sins, repent of them, and submit to the Lordship of Jesus Christ. If you are ready, please prayer this prayer out loud with me:

Lord Jesus, I confess that I am a sinner in need of your forgiveness and grace. I love you and I believe that you are the Son of God. Today, I declare that you are Lord and Savior and king over my life. I believe that the power of sin, death, and the grave is broken over my life. I receive the abundance of grace and the gift of righteousness, and I declare that I reign in life from today and forever. I am a child of God. Amen.

If you have taken the first step to knowing Jesus as your Savior and Lord. The next step is to ask Holy Spirit to come live inside of you so that you can begin to think, live, and act like Jesus. This is called sanctification. Read your Bible, pray, and find a community of believers who can disciple you in the faith. Last, please let me know about your decision by sending me a note on my website at adriennemayfield.com. Welcome to the family!!

Do you feel stuck?

Can't seem to figure out your next move?

Allow Me to Help You Unlock your Destiny!

Visit **adriennemayfield.com** and sign up for your personalized transition coaching session today.

Made in the USA
Monee, IL
25 September 2021